Preventing

Your Staff and Yourself

A Survival Guide for Human Services Supervisors

Rebekah L. Dorman
Jeremy P. Shapiro

CWLA PRESS
WASHINGTON, DC

CWLA Press is an imprint of the Child Welfare League of America. The Child Welfare League of America is the nation's oldest and largest membership-based child welfare organization. We are committed to engaging people everywhere in promoting the well-being of children, youth, and their families, and protecting every child from harm.

© 2004 by the Child Welfare League of America, Inc. All rights reserved. Neither this book nor any part may be reproduced or transmitted in any form or by any means, electronic or mechanical, including photocopying, microfilming, and recording, or by any information storage and retrieval system, without permission in writing from the publisher. For information on this or other CWLA publications, contact the CWLA Publications Department at the address below.

CHILD WELFARE LEAGUE OF AMERICA, INC.
HEADQUARTERS
440 First Street, NW, Third Floor, Washington, DC 20001-2085
E-mail: books@cwla.org

CURRENT PRINTING (last digit)
10 9 8 7 6 5 4 3 2 1

Cover and text design by Amy Alick Perich
Edited by Julie Gwin

Printed in the United States of America

ISBN # 1-58760-003-X

Library of Congress Cataloging-in-Publication Data

Dorman, Rebekah L.
 Preventing burnout in your staff and yourself : a survival guide for human services supervisors / Rebekah L. Dorman and Jeremy P. Shapiro.
   p. cm.
 Includes bibliographical references.
 ISBN 1-58760-003-X (alk. paper)
 1. Human services personnel--Supervision of--Handbooks, manuals, etc. 2. Burn out (Psychology)--Prevention. I. Shapiro, Jeremy P. II. Title.

HV40.54 .D67 2004
658.3'1422--dc22
                                        2003025189

Contents

Dedication v
Acknowledgments vii
A Note to Our Readers..ix

Part 1: Understanding the Components of Job Satisfaction and Burnout..1

    Chapter 1:
    Burnout: An Introduction 3

    Chapter 2:
    What Is Burnout? 7

    Chapter 3:
    Six Dimensions of Job Satisfaction and Burnout..................17

Part 2: Strategies to Prevent Burnout in Your Staff...........39

    Chapter 4:
    Variables that Affect Job Satisfaction and Burnout 41

    Chapter 5:
    Coping Style..47

    Chapter 6:
    Thinking Patterns Associated with Job Satisfaction 53

    Chapter 7:
    A Review and Challenge 63

Suggestions for Further Reading 67
About the Authors 69

Dedication

To Eleanor K. Dorman and Jack Dorman, MD, both of blessed memory, who believed that helping people was the noblest profession.

Acknowledgments

We thank the Ohio Department of Job and Family Services for funding the research on which this manual is largely based and, in particular, Kristin Gilbert of that agency, who provided special assistance on that project. We also thank the professionals who agreed to participate in that research and share their job experiences with us. We acknowledge the members of the Public Children Services Association of Ohio, who participated in a session on job satisfaction and burnout at their annual conference, and Susan Dandareau, Supervisor, Lucas County Children's Services, all of whom graciously shared their ideas and real-life experiences with us. Finally, our thanks to Felicia Shapiro, whose description of her own job experiences helped us understand how to combine realism and optimism.

A Note to Our Readers

We are interested in hearing about your experiences as a supervisor and how you have helped yourself and your staff be resilient and avoid burnout. To share your stories with us, please send e-mail to rldorman@yahoo.com. Thank you!

Part 1

Understanding the Components of Job Satisfaction and Burnout

Chapter 1

Burnout: An Introduction

Carol storms into your office, asking "Can I talk to you for a minute?" as she plops down into the chair opposite your desk. Almost without waiting for an answer, she launches into a detailed summary of a case that has gone wrong at every turn and has finally "blown up." The local hospital has just notified her of another serious abuse incident. She is on her way to the emergency room to talk with the parents and remove the children from the home for the third time. She is angry, frustrated, and just plain tired of dealing with the parents, who keep failing to follow through on the case plan, and the judge, who continues to send the children back to the family, despite her recommendations. Carol ends her story and then looks up at you. You have vague memories of this case, but you supervise a number of workers and hear about many such cases. She is looking to you to help her cope with the torrent of feelings she is facing and help her be most effective when she goes to the hospital to manage this crisis.

What Do You Do?

As a supervisor in the human services, an agency calls on you to deal with a variety of personnel issues related to the staff under your supervision. None is more challenging than coping with a staff person who is in the midst of emotional turmoil, such as Carol, the worker in the previous scenario. Carol has not yet burned out, but she may be on her way if her supervisor does not help her manage her feelings and cope effectively with this and other similarly stressful situations. Worker burnout is one of the most serious and potentially destructive problems you face.

Burned-out workers experience both psychological and physiological symptoms that result in lowered productivity and effectiveness, use of more sick leave and, ultimately, job turnover. Its effects are far reaching, affecting not only you and your supervisee, but also clients and the human services field as a whole.

No quick and easy answers to the problem of professional burnout exist. Researchers have recognized the issue as a serious one for several decades and have conducted a number of studies to investigate the problem and also its opposite, job satisfaction. This research has produced significant insights into both the problem and its potential solutions. This manual applies the research to your job as a supervisor and offers you tools for an important aspect of your job: helping prevent burnout and enhance job satisfaction in your supervisees.

The word *burnout* has entered the everyday English language, but we in the helping professions have the dubious distinction of originating the term. The phenomenon of burnout was first noticed, and has received most of its research attention, in the human services fields of child welfare and mental health. Burnout, also known as "compassion fatigue," seems to be an occupational hazard of jobs devoted to helping people who are experiencing serious problems.

No more difficult type of work exists in the world. We try and try and try, but nonetheless, we experience obstacles and difficulties. Sometimes we fail, and sometimes the people we want to help do not even appreciate our efforts. Sometimes we feel as if we are battering our heads against a wall. We give and give to our clients, put our heart into our work, and get little in return.

And yet, we know people who have stayed in the field for many years and remain committed and energized: It is possible. Why are some people able to avoid burnout and remain satisfied with their jobs? In our search for answers, it makes sense to use the tools of our field—figuring people out and devising solutions based on our understanding to help us find the answers. Throughout this manual, we turn to our research findings, the research of others, and the experiences of real workers and supervisors for guidance on how to handle situations like the one presented above. We offer suggestions for how to create an overall workplace environment that supports job satisfaction, as well as more specific suggestions about dealing with your staff, including how to make sure that

Burnout: An Introduction

your limited supervision time with your staff is used to best advantage. Although clearly many factors are not under your control at work, we believe that most of the suggestions we offer are not "pie in the sky" ideas, but practical pointers that can be put to use immediately.

Chapter 2 | What Is Burnout?

It's Monday morning. In walks Barbara Burnout holding a huge Styrofoam cup of coffee and looking half asleep as she trudges to her desk. She gives you a grudging hello, dumps her things on her desk, and takes the first two hours of the day to figure out her schedule for the week. Barbara blames the paperwork demands, difficult families, and bureaucratic obstacles for her low productivity.

Coming in behind her is Jessica Job Satisfaction, stepping lively and giving you a genuine smile and hello. Within five minutes of sitting down at her desk, she is on the phone confirming appointments she made last week, and within an hour, she is out the door and on her the way to meet with a family. Jessica's productivity is often above 100% of her goal, she sometimes works extra hours to ensure that she meets her goal, and she doesn't complain about it.

Can you relate to the two prototypical staff people described above? Most supervisors know burnout when they see it and dread supervision time with those burned-out staff, even though it is precisely those staff who can benefit from supervision most of all. Without a clear plan on how to help these employees, however, supervision may be a depressing time of listening to the worker's complaints and excuses and observing his or her ineffectiveness with families. It is our hope that this manual will provide you with some ideas for making supervision time one of the keys to helping staff recover from burnout.

Freudenberger coined the term *burnout* in 1974 to describe the emotional exhaustion and decreased work motivation often experienced by human service professionals. Professionals who are burned out feel emotionally exhausted and worn down by their jobs. The experience of work is miserable for them. Burned-out workers watch the clock and long for the end of the work day. Burnout could be defined as depression on the job.

Burnout occurs over time and is a gradual process, eroding one's motivation to achieve and emotional connection with clients. Along the way often comes the development of physical symptoms, such as chronic fatigue, headaches, stomach problems, or backaches. Abuse of alcohol or drugs may also occur.

Avoidance of work is a central feature of burnout, which manifests itself in varying degrees. Professionals with a strong sense of responsibility force themselves to put in the appropriate number of hours, but their motivation erodes, their efficiency is impaired, and they find themselves wasting time on extraneous activities because almost anything feels better than concentrating on work.

The burnout syndrome includes depersonalization of clients—staff avoid emotional connection with their clients, lose awareness of the clients' individuality and suffering, and come to see all clients as being the same. When this syndrome progresses, work avoidance becomes more blatant. Burnout is associated with calling in sick and, ultimately, quitting one's job and leaving the human service field.

For the most part, high job satisfaction is the opposite of burnout. Professionals with high job satisfaction enjoy their work, put a lot of effort into their jobs, and remain in their fields. They find their jobs interesting and worthwhile.

Job satisfaction is composed of a number of distinct components that together make up a worker's overall attitude toward his or her job. People who are satisfied with one aspect of their job tend to be pleased with other aspects. Although it is not universally true that satisfied workers are effective in their jobs, usually this is the case. Such professionals are engaged and invested in the work they do, take pride in their accomplishments, and feel energetic as they approach their day.

The Stressors of Human Services Work

It is not difficult to understand why work in the field of child maltreatment can produce high rates of caseworker burnout. Coming into contact with child abuse and neglect causes shock, anger, and sadness in professionals and nonprofessionals alike. In fact, given the high levels of stress inherent in child welfare work, it seems surprising that some workers avoid burnout and stay in the field for years.

What Is Burnout?

> *Ms. S. has completed her case plan successfully. She attended the parenting and anger management classes and has found a new boyfriend who seems upbeat and supportive. She participates in regular visits with her two small children and is looking forward to being reunified with them. Jeff, their caseworker, recommends that it is time to reunify the family, and the judge agrees. Finally, the day arrives, and Jeff watches the happy reunion of parent and children. He feels some pride that his work on this case helped to make this day possible. Three months later, he learns that the children are back in the system. Jeff is left to wonder how he could have been so wrong about this case and questions his professional judgment.*

Demoralization involves many individual factors and takes many forms. Some professionals experience a sense of helplessness, as their years of efforts seem to make no dent in the societal problem of child maltreatment. Many are debilitated by chronic feelings of anger—toward offenders, the system, or nonoffending parents who fail to protect their children. Many doubt their own competence when cases go poorly and are troubled by feelings of inadequacy and low self-esteem. As these stressors and responses to them accumulate, a professional may become cynical, hopeless, and simply exhausted—this is burnout. The result is impaired professional effectiveness, low job satisfaction, and sometimes, leaving the helping professions.

Jobs in community mental health often produce similar experiences, partly because the client populations are largely the same. Work with multiproblem families confronts professionals with a seemingly endless series of barriers, frustrations, and setbacks. The children are hurting and in desperate need, and we respond with recommendations that seem capable of helping, but so many things can go wrong. Practical or systems factors may make it impossible to implement the case plan. Personal problems in the parents may derail their implementation of positive strategies, and families sometimes absorb a great deal of intervention without showing any positive effects.

> *Antoine's defiant, aggressive behavior was gradually brought under control by a combination of family therapy and parent guidance. After some initial resistance, Antoine said he loved his behavior chart because "it teaches me how to act right," and his mom said, "He wants to be good, but he needed help to know how." Jane, the therapist, was thrilled with this progress. Then, a boyfriend entered the picture who believed the new*

> practices were spoiling the child. Jane asked the boyfriend to join in the therapy sessions, but his response was that he did not believe in therapy. The family soon dropped out of treatment and would not return phone calls. Jane felt was certain that all of the hard work that she and this family had done together was now being destroyed by a man she had never met. She envisioned Antoine's aggressive behavior escalating and eventually landing him in jail or getting him killed.

Human services work is emotionally stressful by its nature. New workers quickly meet the realities of human services work and may be confronted by an array of difficult situations. Providers repeatedly come into close contact with the suffering of innocent children and adults. When professionals internalize their clients' traumatic memories, the result is "vicarious traumatization." Years of such experiences sometimes result in compassion fatigue in even the most caring of professionals, who feel their resources have been used up and they have nothing left to give.

> Mr. and Mrs. R. often miss their scheduled visits with their children, and when they do make the visit, their behavior is mostly negative and punitive. The children are so upset after each visit that the foster mother says it takes them a week to calm back down. All of the professionals involved in the case tell the judge that permanent custody should be granted to the state, but the judge decides to continue the case because Mr. and Mrs. R. plead with him for one more chance. Kristin, the foster care case manager, leaves the courthouse worrying about how this will affect the kids, how she will tell the foster parents who are eager to adopt the children, and feeling generally helpless to move the case along to a successful resolution.

The stressors are distressingly common, and many carry devastating consequences for children and families:

- An investigation fails to determine what happened, so that the child returns to an abusive situation.
- Family members do not cooperate with the investigation and appear to be protecting the perpetrator instead of the child.

> As I interviewed the grandmother of a toddler who lay in intensive care from being thrown against a wall, she asked me why I was making such a big deal out of "this unfortunate incident." She seemed more worried about protecting her son than whether her granddaughter would recover.

What Is Burnout?

I felt a cold rage inside of me and wondered how I would be able to work with her in the future.

- The evidence seems clear, but the system fails the child.
- Caseloads are large, and it is difficult to spend adequate time with each family.
- A case with a tragic ending hits the media, causing everyone to be on edge.

I am working with a very depressed mother who—no kidding—looks just like Andrea Yates. She seems to be able to accept the support I offer, and yet I keep asking myself, could she do something horrible to the kids?

- Funding is inadequate, and workers cannot provide desperately needed services.
- Families refuse to cooperate with the case plan and show little interest in their children, but appear at court hearings begging to have their children returned—and the judge gives them another chance.
- The family successfully completes their case plan, and the child is returned, but in a short time is abused again.

Every time a bad outcome occurs with a child or family I feel awful and wonder whether I should stay in this field. But I don't feel like I can abandon work that is so important and meaningful.

- A child client's acting-out behavior rises and falls with her mother's drug use; the counselor repeatedly offers the mother a referral for treatment, and she agrees to get help, but she never follows through.
- A child's anxiety disorder seems due largely to his parents' repeated threats to send him to a foster home if he misbehaves; despite the therapist's efforts, the parents continue the threats because they believe this keeps the child in line.

Often I can see what could be done to help a family with a problem, but then other problems make it impossible to do what would help. What do you do when every potential solution is blocked by a different problem?

These factors are stressors that make the job experience difficult for caseworkers. A stressor is not the same thing as a defeat, however. Workers may view stressors as challenges that can overwhelm them or that they can master, or at least manage. The key to surviving stress—whether at work or anywhere else—is coping. The individual's coping in response to a stressor determines the effect of that external situation or event. If coping is unsuccessful, these stressors can take a serious toll on professional caseworkers.

Your Role as Supervisor

My friend, Frank, became a supervisor about a year after I did. Within a few weeks of his promotion, he came complaining to me about how he had to reprimand a staff person who wasn't following agency policies, deal with employee complaints, and figure out how to mollify a nasty parent who was complaining about a staff person. Frank had been an excellent caseworker, but he was always somewhat critical of management prior to his promotion. "Welcome to the dark side," I told him, only half joking. "This is what being a manager is all about."

It is likely that your fine work with families was the reason for your promotion to supervisor, and yet this is the one thing you do not do as a supervisor. Suddenly, you are placed on the other side of the desk, doling out assignments, evaluating staff performance, listening to disgruntled employees, and trying to explain the needs of your staff to upper management while enforcing upper management's decisions with your staff. It is unlikely that you received much, if any, training for this new role. Many supervisors feel unprepared for the emotional toll that this new role takes on them as they struggle to do the balancing act called middle management. This struggle occurs in an environment in which children's lives are at stake. You are not trying to sell more breakfast cereal or make a better widget, you are trying to keep children safe and help families heal.

In addition to managing your own stress, you must support your staff in their role with children and families. As you know from your own experience, this can take an enormous toll. How can you manage your own stress successfully and help your staff manage theirs, so that burnout is averted and job satisfaction is maintained or even increased? How do you support and nurture resilient workers who cope well with the constant challenges that are endemic to this work?

You are left either to draw on your personal experiences with your own supervisors or to search out other models of supervision, if your personal experiences were not happy ones. But who has time to read textbooks on management philosophy? And how relevant are mass market advice books that focus on a business environment? That is why we wrote this handbook. Our suggestions are evidence based and drawn from the world of human services, and are much more about practical advice than about philosophical frameworks.

What Is Resilience in Human Services Work?

Over the past 20 years, there has been increasing interest in understanding how some children living in stressful, high-risk situations are able to succeed against the odds and become happy, productive adults. Research (Egeland, Carlson, & Sroufe, 1993; Werner, 1993) has identified factors both in the child and the environment that are common in resilient children. This research is important to our work with children and families, because it provides insight into how to increase our clients' resilience in the face of stressful, potentially harmful environments.

In addition, this research is important because parallels between resilience in children and burnout prevention in human services professionals exist: Both are about coping successfully with difficult, painful situations. The research we did on job satisfaction helps us understand how certain professionals operating in very stressful working conditions are able to maintain a productive, positive attitude toward their work. As in the research on resilient children, certain factors in the individual contribute to being a resilient worker, but factors in the environment are also extremely important. As a supervisor, you can control or shape many of those factors through your relationship with your staff and through ability to control or modify aspects of the work environment in which they operate.

It seems clear some stressors are unlikely to dissipate because they are inherent in the work, so our goal as supervisors is to help staff people navigate those stormy waters and not capsize in the inevitable storms that they will face. The resilient worker will be able to move on and meet the next challenge ahead. Their failures will not become defeats, but experiences to learn from and stories to share with others.

The Nature of the Supervisory Relationship

As a supervisor, you wield power, and supervisees recognize that fact, but we hope they are not intimidated by it. Your goal should not be dominance and control, but leadership in a shared learning experience, in which you and the worker are partners with a common mission: to protect and help children and families. The sign of a successful partnership is that both supervisor and supervisee feel enriched by their relationship and come away from their supervisory sessions with a sense of accomplishment. This feeling of accomplishment can occur if you have set up supervision as a way of learning from failures as well as celebrating successes. This is truly easier said than done, especially when children's lives and well-being are at stake, but one of the lessons learned through research is that without that attitude, burnout becomes a real risk. The fact is that failures will occur, so how one deals with those failures is crucial.

Supervising is a little like parenting. From research and clinical practice, we have learned that authoritative parenting produces the most competent and happiest children (Baumrind, 1967). In this parenting style, the adult uses a combination of warmth and nurturance along with an appropriate amount of structure or control to guide the child. Authoritative supervising, which both nurtures your staff and maintains appropriate expectations and structure, is likely to result in a happy and productive supervisory relationship in which the staff person feels both supported and pushed to excel.

The Research

In articles published in the *Journal of Child Sexual Abuse* (Shapiro, Burkey, Dorman, & Welker, 1996; Shapiro, Dorman, Burkey, & Welker, 1999), we described our research on job satisfaction and burnout in professionals who work with abused children. We administered several questionnaires to 215 professionals attending a training on child sexual abuse. The participants came from a variety of disciplines—mostly child welfare and mental health, and also education, juvenile justice, and nursing. We found that patterns of burnout and job satisfaction were similar across disciplines, and so we reported results for the sample as a whole.

The study involved three main assessment measures. One questionnaire measured job satisfaction and burnout. We designed this instrument specifically for professionals who work with abused children and their families. Another instrument assessed the respondent's style of coping with stressors at work. The third measure assessed cognitions concerning work with abused children and their families; this measure assessed perceptions, attitudes, beliefs, and thoughts related to this work.

The research strategy was to examine relationships among these three variables: job satisfaction and burnout, coping strategies, and work-related cognitions. The first question was whether professionals' coping strategies and work-related cognitions make a difference to their level of burnout. The answer to this question was, definitely, yes. The next, more complicated question was, in what ways? In other words, we wanted to identify the specific coping strategies and work-related thoughts that were associated with high levels of job satisfaction and those that were associated with high levels of burnout.

References

Baumrind, D. (1967). Child-care practices anteceding three patterns of preschool behavior. *Genetic Psychology Monographs*, 75, 43–88.

Egeland, B., Carlson, E., & Sroufe, L. A. (1993). Resilience as process. *Development and Psychopathology*, 5, 517–528.

Shapiro, J. P., Burkey, W. B., Dorman, R. L., & Welker, C. J. (1996). Job satisfaction and burnout in child abuse professionals: Measure development, factor analysis, and job characteristics. *Journal of Child Sexual Abuse,* 5, 21–38.

Shapiro, J. P., Dorman, R. L., Burkey, W. B., & Welker, C. J. (1999). Predictors of job satisfaction and burnout in child abuse professionals: Coping, cognition, and victimization history. *Journal of Child Sexual Abuse,* 7, 23–42.

Werner, E. E. (1993). Risk, resilience, and recovery: Perspectives from the Kauai Longitudinal Study. *Development and Psychopathology*, 5, 503–515.

Chapter 3: Six Dimensions of Job Satisfaction and Burnout

The first goal of the study described in Chapter 2 was to understand the components or ingredients of job satisfaction. The question was, What is job satisfaction made of? We used a statistical procedure called factor analysis to break job satisfaction down into its basic parts. The results provide information about the anatomy or structure of work experience for professionals who work with abused children and their families.

The analysis revealed six main dimensions or components of job satisfaction:

- self-actualization
- environmental support for achievement
- job-related affect
- working conditions
- professional self-esteem
- futility/avoidance

When these factors are at positive levels, they compose high job satisfaction, and when they are at negative levels, the result is burnout. These components are described in the order of importance as indicated by the statistical analysis, starting with the most important dimension.

Factor 1: Self-Actualization

The most important factor in job satisfaction revealed by our research is self-actualization. The items in this factor all refer to abstract, high-level sources of satisfaction, as opposed to more basic, everyday needs. Self-actualization is about becoming more than we initially are by exercising our capabilities and developing new skills. Self-actualization is about personal ideals, values, creativity, and growth. In the questionnaire, the items related to self-actualization concerned professional skill development, intellectual stimulation and learning, a sense of meaningful connection with clients, and making a contribution to the lives of other people.

Satisfied workers tended to agree, and burned-out workers tended to disagree, with items like:

- My work is intellectually interesting.
- My job involves continued learning and development of my skills.
- I feel I make an important contribution to people's lives with the work I do.

Additional results corroborated the importance of intellectual stimulation and professional learning in job satisfaction. Although educational degrees were unrelated to work satisfaction, continuing education emerged as important: The more trainings workers attended, and the more articles and books they read, the happier they were with their jobs.

It was surprising to discover that self-actualization was the most important single factor in determining levels of job satisfaction in the sample of human service professionals. But this finding does make sense if we are clear about what it does and does not mean: The finding was not that the sample had high levels of self-actualization. Instead, we found that whether or not professionals were satisfied with their jobs depended more on their level of self-actualization at work than on any other single factor.

In the sample, highly satisfied workers tended to have work-related motives that were largely growth oriented, intellectual, and humanistic. With the large workloads and extensive paperwork requirements of child welfare work, nothing is more natural than spending all of one's time immersed in the process of getting tasks done and avoiding mistakes; it can be difficult to find the time to step back and think about the larger issues involved in this work. Nonetheless, our results indicate that work experiences are more positive for professionals who do sometimes think about the big picture, including the interesting, difficult questions involved in their work, the professional skills they use, and the ways their work benefits children and families.

Some professionals bring this intellectual curiosity with them to their job, and supervisors simply need to find ways to allow it to be expressed and nurtured. This is an enviable task for the supervisor. The much more difficult job for the supervisor presents itself in the form of the employee who just wants to make it through the week and never expresses an interest in learning, developing, contributing, or self-actualizing. Nonetheless, it might may be possible to spark the interest of some of these staff, and this chapter presents some ideas. After all, we are in this field because of our belief that people can change.

Implications for Supervisors

Supervisors can help their staff members rise above the routinized aspect of work by introductions like the following: "Let's think about what we know about child therapy/development/protection in general and then see how that knowledge applies to this particular case." He or she can ask significant questions, for example:

- What are the indicators that a child's allegation is valid?
- What are the risk factors for future abuse?
- How can we judge the likelihood that a given intervention will have a positive effect on a parent's caregiving difficulties?
- What are the specific skill components in effective case management?
- How has this family changed in the course of their child protective services (CPS) involvement?
- What might have happened if CPS involvement had not occurred?
- What are the cognitive and emotional processes in the child that have contributed to his or her difficulties? How could therapy address those processes?
- What are the family systems or environmental factors that have led to the development of these problems? How could I address those factors?
- What does outcome research say about the therapeutic strategies most likely to help children with the client's array of problems, needs, and strengths?

- What are the strengths or partial solutions already present in the family that could become foundations for further growth and problem resolution?

The recommendation is not that supervisors spend hours and hours philosophizing with their supervisees; that would not be practical, nor is it necessary. But weaving scientific or conceptual thinking into supervision and reflecting on what can be learned from the cases at hand strengthens the effectiveness of planning and develops supervisee skills. This type of supervision brings immediate benefits to the services provided to the clients under discussion. In addition, staff members who feel that their jobs involve learning and development—that is, self-actualization—have more interest and enthusiasm for their work. A few minutes of reflecting on the connections between cases and the larger issues they raise can elevate the experience of all the rest of the hours in the week.

Highlight and create opportunities for learning and skill development. Set up a lunch discussion group to talk about a case study or article. This is an opportunity to develop a norm where staff feel comfortable batting around ideas, entertaining different approaches to cases, and discussing approaches used in other settings. Staff may be timid at first, so supervisors can begin by presenting cases from their days in the field. It is important to be able to discuss failures to demonstrate how to make use of these experiences and to learn from them. The point to get across is how to take the lessons from that case and apply them to others.

Sometimes staff get so enmeshed in a case that they can recite each family member's history in frightening detail—and start to explain the case to you in supervision with such a detailed description that it is hard to understand the overall dynamics of the case. Multiproblem families with stories that could top any soap opera plotline are commonplace in child welfare and mental health work. Do not allow staff to get mired in the sordid details if these are not relevant to the work they are doing with the family now. Help them by asking big picture questions such as, "Is there a key component of the system in which change might produce positive ripple effects?", "What would be positive ways for each person to get what he wants?", "What has worked best with this family so far?" "What is their greatest strength?", and "How does the family view you?"

The key to high-quality learning experiences at work seems to be connecting general knowledge to specific cases. Such connections can go in either direction: When discussing individual cases, it is useful to ask about the general principles that apply and, when discussing theory or research, it is useful to think about specific cases germane to those concepts or findings. Theory without connection to real human experience is dry, whereas case material without conceptualization is impossible to organize and comprehend. The combination of general and specific thinking is the essence of applying knowledge. When staff see a connection between the family they saw last Tuesday and an idea cited by their supervisor or colleague, they participate in their field's overarching endeavor to understand and help families, and this increases self-actualization and job satisfaction.

How to Present a Case

Staff may need to be trained on how to present a case effectively. Some basic guidelines for what to include are:

- Description of the core features of the child's and family's difficulties and strengths, with a few illustrative details to help the group picture the clients.
- Presentation of a succinct narrative, including the most important events of the story.
- An attempt to explain why the problems developed, with consideration of at least one theoretical framework relevant to the case.
- Citation of outcome research or, if none exists, expert opinion that points toward intervention strategies for which some basis of confidence exists.
- Citation of the clinical or practical thinking of the worker and supervisor concerning the intervention options available that seem most likely to succeed.

To be enjoyable and effective, case presentations need to strike a balance between support for all participants and a lively exchange of ideas. Staff will not be willing to venture their thoughts if a danger of being put down by other participants exists, and managers need to facilitate an atmosphere of respect for all opinions. At the same time, discussions consisting of nothing but mutual agreement are dull and less than maximally educational; discussions are most interesting and useful when some controversy exists and different ideas are brought into contact with each other. Such discussions leave participants feeling stimulated, curious, and, if intimidated by the mysteries of the work, at least engaged in the lifelong process of unraveling those mysteries.

It will be a real bonus if the agency can provide lunch to staff or if supervisors pitch in together to underwrite the cost. Pizza is always a cost-effective choice. This will encourage staff who may not otherwise attend to do so. Food is also, of course, a tangible way of expressing nurturance to your staff.

Provide Intellectual Perspective by Discussing Major Issues

In the press of day-to-day work, it is easy to lose the forest for the trees, but our results indicate that people are happier in their work when they also have some awareness of the forest. In each case, no matter how unusual, will be some issue or lesson that workers can look at in a broader context. Each case can be a learning opportunity. Some cases, in which the family history is beyond the situations portrayed in the most outlandish tabloid television show, may seem hard to draw generalizations from, yet workers can always extract some kernel that can be applied to another case. For example, they could learn how to manage complex cases with many different areas of pathology or how to look for strengths in a family that appears to have few.

This type of exercise can add an important component to a worker's sense of everyday mission. We all need to get our work done, and sometimes overwhelming piles of it exist, but job satisfaction is maximized when people also have a sense of themselves as trying to learn, figure out the mysteries, and so do the job a little bit better the next time. Intellectual curiosity adds spice to what otherwise can become a dull daily grind.

Encourage Creative Approaches

Professionals with high job satisfaction feel they use their creative abilities in their jobs. Some of your staff may be able to do this naturally, and your work with them is to reward their creativity. Professionals who are effective in providing community-based services, especially services in the home, are generally able to think creatively, flexibly, and on the spot.

> *I had been working with Shannon, an adolescent girl in foster care, for a number of months. She went into a panic each time she had to take a test in school and would become overwrought as she struggled to answer the*

test questions. I had taught her a deep breathing exercise to help relax her, but she insisted that she didn't have time to do it during a test, displaying an adolescent stubbornness that had tested my skill as a change agent. I sat and thought for a minute and asked, "Do you think you could take a deep breath every time you turned the page of the test?" She agreed that she could. I don't know how I came up with that idea, but I felt an incredible sense of triumph that I had finally gotten Shannon to agree to try something new.

Jesse was 5 and terrified of monsters. With his abusive history, it was no wonder that he had trouble sleeping. His foster parents were at the end of their rope, since they had not gotten a decent night's sleep since his arrival in their home. On one visit to the foster home, I saw a spray bottle the foster mother used to water plants, and suddenly I had an idea. I returned in a couple days with an empty spray bottled labeled "Monster Spray." I explained to Jesse that this special spray kept monsters away from his bed. Together we went to his room, and he sprayed all around his bed. From that day on, visits from monsters were much reduced.

For the staff member who consistently gets stuck, who meets a resistant client and throws up his or her hands, your task is obviously more difficult. You may suggest different approaches to a situation and model creative thinking. You may also need to be creative in figuring out how to help this worker progress in her thinking. Does it help to question him or her? How about giving an example from another case? This will be a process of shaping the staff person's behavior, helping them loosen up, and pushing them to go beyond standard procedures.

Emphasize Workers' Positive Effects on Families

The multiproblem dysfunctional families with whom your staff spend much, if not most, of their time can appear hopeless. Some will resist any offer of help, shrug off any support, and be unresponsive to confrontation. But many others will be able to accept help and make real changes in their lives. Perhaps the changes will be small, and the family may be far from optimal in their lifestyle and parenting practices. But do they scream *less,* do they hit *less,* do they praise *more*? Family functioning exists on a continuum, and the families with whom we work are at the lower end of that continuum. Helping the family move a notch toward optimal is an accomplishment and should be recognized. We have reason to believe that when families make some changes, however small, other changes will probably follow.

Your staff, especially those members with little experience, need to gain this small-change perspective to be resilient. Seeing those small, positive steps is crucial to being able to continue to work successfully with a family.

> *When I was green, I thought success meant that, following my caseplan, a parent had gone through parenting classes and therapy and had become a warm and loving parent to their kids. Now, if a parent even agrees to go see a therapist, I'm pleased. In fact, some days my biggest success is that every family has let me in the door.*

Factor 2: Achievement Support

The next most important factor in job satisfaction, and the aspect of the external work environment most important to social service professionals, is interpersonal support and enhancement of performance and achievement, particularly from supervisors. Achievement support involves a combination of interpersonal issues and achievement issues; this factor concerns enhancement of job performance by relationships with people and the social structure of work. Achievement support is the component of job satisfaction most directly related to the supervisory relationship.

Highly satisfied workers tended to agree with statements like:

- My supervisor's expectations of me are clear.
- My supervisor is knowledgeable, skillful, and helpful to me in my work.
- I get clear feedback from my supervisor about my work.
- I have about the right amount of independence in my work.
- I get a lot of support and social enjoyment from my colleagues at work.

In general, the items concern the degree to which the social structures of the work environment support quality performance. The supervisory relationship is central to these items, but it is important to note that the issue is not the closeness or warmth of relationships, but rather facilitation of professional achievement by the supervisor. Providers want to receive the tools, information, and independence they need to do an optimal job, and then they want clear feedback on how they are doing so that they can make further improvements. Feedback is probably most useful when it includes a mix of positive evaluation and suggested avenues for improvement.

Implications for Supervisors

Be a Teacher

> At our peer meeting, I watched as the supervisor monopolized the discussion by peppering the staff person making the case presentation with question after question. What was worse was that almost before the worker had a chance to answer, the supervisor had given her opinion of the situation. None of the other workers said a word at the meeting. It was clear that the supervisor had become so involved with the case that she had forgotten that these meetings were designed to strengthen staff's clinical skills, not for her to micromanage cases.

The supervisor described above realized after the meeting that she had made a mistake and set out to correct it. At the next peer meeting, her questions were open-ended and focused mostly on eliciting the staff's opinions on the case. She asked questions like, "Do you agree with the psychiatrist's diagnosis?" and " What do you plan to do next?", whereas in the first meeting, she had focused on the details of the case. Staff responded well and began to offer opinions and talk with each other. Their body language was completely different from the first meeting, in which arms were folded, gazes averted, and mouths held together in a tense, pursed expression. In the second meeting, staff leaned forward, appeared relaxed, and spoke with animation.

Offer Specific Suggestions for Cases

At times it is appropriate to make direct, specific suggestions about a case, in terms of understanding the family dynamics, making a diagnosis, or planning effective interventions. After all, presumably a large part of why you were promoted to the supervisory level is your skill level with families.

Go into the Field with Staff

In certain cases, it will be helpful for you to meet with a client or family yourself, along with your supervisee. It may be that the staff person feels threatened or uncomfortable when visiting that home or meeting with that client, and he or she requires your support and guidance in person. Your willingness to go into the field and experience what the worker has been experiencing will be a huge morale booster, and you are likely to gain some important insights into how to move this case along. It is good practice to go into the field with staff periodically even without the impetus of an extremely difficult case.

Be a Helper as Well as a Boss

Supporting the performance and achievement level of supervisees is a primary aspect of the supervisor's job. By providing useful information, help with skill enhancement, clear expectations, and plenty of feedback about performance, supervisors offer their staff opportunities for professional growth at work, and these opportunities, in turn, contribute to staff's satisfaction with their jobs.

Be accessible to supervisees, and have regular supervision scheduled. Time is a valuable commodity in a fast-paced environment, but repeatedly canceling supervision communicates to your staff that your time with them falls in last place in your priorities. Of course, at times, emergencies will intervene, but make this the exception and not the rule. To the greatest extent possible, supervision time should be a protected time, free from interruptions and phone calls. Reserving this time for staff is the most tangible way for you to send the message that they are important and valued by you.

Provide Clear Expectations and Clear Feedback on Performance

Providing clear expectations to a supervisee should be done most formally during the annual evaluation with agreed-on goals for the next year listed in the evaluation document. On an ongoing basis, your staff should clearly understand tasks assigned to them, and if the tasks are time sensitive, you should give them a deadline. Having basic written office procedures for the worker to follow is extremely helpful so that supervision time can be spent in a more effective way, by discussing cases. E-mail is a fast, easy tool for communicating ongoing assignments, and it leaves behind a written record for both sender and recipient.

Allow Appropriate Independence

Don't look over supervisees' shoulders more than necessary. To learn to make judgments and function as a skilled professional, staff should not be micromanaged. On the other hand, when the judgments are considered critical, such as emergency removal of a child from a home, consultation with a supervisor or a team of peers and a supervisor may be the better route. So many gray areas exist in our work, yet so many highly emotional situations require a black or white decision. Should the child remain in this home? Should you recommend reunification? Should the child be hospitalized? Should you make a report? By providing back-up in decisionmaking, the staff person never feels out on a limb.

Encourage Staff to Learn from Each Other

The achievement support factor included items referring to positive relationships with colleagues as well as with supervisors. Combining this aspect of job satisfaction with the earlier finding about self-actualization suggests that creating forums in which staff teach and learn from each other might be a particularly effective way to promote positive job experiences.

Educational experiences seem most interesting and useful when they connect the intellectual aspects of work—research, theory, and reading—with the practical aspects, namely, real work with real clients. One effective way to do this is to arrange for seminar-like staff meetings, in which one professional presents both a case and some research with direct applicability to that case. For instance, if the central issue of the case is parental noncompliance, the worker could present some research on working with resistant parents, and if the client's presenting problems are reactions to sexual victimization, someone could present research on treating posttraumatic stress disorder. Applying research-based knowledge to everyday clinical challenges brings providers the benefits of other people's hard-won discoveries. From a job satisfaction perspective, instituting a series of monthly case conferences with a genuine educational component would harness both the self-actualization and achievement support factors to enhance participants' work experiences.

Encourage Staff to Support Each Other

When staff return from a difficult home visit or session with a client, they cannot expect to debrief with their supervisor immediately. Supervisors cannot always be available to staff. Staff members may have some very strong feelings or concerns about a case, however, and need to talk with someone to process them. Their peers in the office can provide this much-needed daily support. By encouraging staff to debrief as needed with each other, you build the staff into a team who support and nurture each other.

> *I had to break the very bad news to Christine, my newest and youngest staff member, that a child on her caseload had died. We didn't have any details beyond that. I knew this was a favorite family of hers, and she had talked about this baby with affection. Then I had to run to a meeting that I couldn't miss. Before I left, I approached another member of my staff, the most senior person on the unit, and asked her to check in on Christine in the next few minutes and lend her support. I learned upon my return that Christine had, indeed, broken down with that staff person, once the shock had worn off. But she felt greatly comforted by [the staff person's] presence and the sharing of her own experience with a child on her caseload who had died.*

Factor 3: Job-Related Affect

The third most important factor was job-related affect. These items describe the participants' emotional experiences of their jobs, and the items are easily recognized by the emotion descriptors in their wording, for instance, "upset," "depressed," and "exhausting." Both positive and negative emotions are involved in these items. Satisfied professionals tended to agree with statements like, "I am eager to go to work each day." Burned-out workers tended to agree with statements like, "I am often upset and depressed by my clients' problems."

The emotional experience of work is the end result of processes involving the job environment and the individual's way of thinking about and coping with work challenges. Probably the most important way to intervene helpfully with regard to the affect factor is to work through the other factors, however, some ways to help make the emotional environment of the workplace positive and pleasant exist.

Implications for Supervisors

Have Dress Up and Dress Down Days

On designated days, allow staff to wear special types of clothing. For example, one public agency allowed staff to dress up for Halloween and other holidays as part of an intensive retention campaign. These and other measures resulted in a dramatic increase in staff job satisfaction and reduction in turnover.

Another agency holds "spirit days" and has staff dress for themes such as hobbies, favorite sports teams, and so on. If the agency maintains a dress code that precludes blue jeans and other casual dress, give staff the opportunity to wear that clothing (within reason) periodically.

Plan Social Events

A summer barbeque, a fall retreat, and a winter holiday party, all with food and fun supplied by the agency, can really lift spirits and send an institutional message that employees are valued. Such events also allow staff to interact with each other in fun, relaxed surroundings, providing a welcome break from the usually highly charged atmosphere in which staff normally see each other.

Give Staff a Variety of Assignments

By giving staff some duties that are less emotionally taxing and also that develop other talents, a supervisor provides them with a broader perspective on their work and the agency and gives them a break from regular client-related duties. For example, depending on each person's strengths, assign them to a speaker's bureau, have them serve on various committees in the agency, assign them to serve as liaison to another agency, put them in charge of planning an agency event, and so forth.

An additional benefit of having line staff serve on administrative committees is that they gain some insight into the types of issues supervisors and administrators must manage on a daily basis. This allows them to place management decisions into context and demystifies, to some degree, the workings of upper management, which workers sometimes perceive as distant, aloof, and uncaring of line staff.

Factor 4: Working Conditions

The next factor is called working conditions. Whereas the achievement support factor concerned the social environment of work, this factor is about the practical, concrete job environment and whether it supports or hinders work effectiveness and satisfaction. Both physical characteristics of the office and burdensomeness of procedures are part of the working conditions factor. This is a simple factor with straightforward questions

about the job environment. Example items include:
- The office environment at my agency is pleasant.
- A great deal of unnecessary paperwork exists at my job.

It is interesting to note that in this study, no differences existed between public agency child welfare workers and the rest of the sample on five of the six job satisfaction factors; the one exception was the working conditions factor. Public agency workers produced lower scores on this section than the other professionals who worked with sexually abused children and their families. This may be because funding constraints limit what can be spent to make the physical conditions of work attractive and convenient, and because the extensive regulations involved in human services work result in large paperwork requirements, which can be burdensome for caseworkers.

Child welfare work is regulated by local, state, and federal authorities, and therefore comes replete with rules and paperwork. No one goes into child welfare work saying, "I'm really looking forward to doing lots of paperwork and dealing with all of those regulations." (The people who feel that way tend to go into quality improvement.) The result is that staff members who are dedicated to saving children have to document their work in a somewhat tedious fashion and probably hate every minute of it. Your role as supervisor is to help them abide by the rules and regulations and help them see the rules as the means to an end—helping people.

Implications for Supervisors

Make Paperwork User Friendly

Although paperwork is a fact of life, ways to improve and consolidate forms and procedures so that they are less cumbersome do exist. Streamlining paperwork by assessing whether each form is really necessary and whether all the information on the form is needed, and eliminating redundancies in forms and the information gathering procedures will produce better-quality records. A supervisor can make forms user friendly by talking with staff about the layout of the form and problems completing it.

> We made the very simple change of adding the title of each form at the bottom of the page in addition to the top. Our records are bound together at the top and the old way meant either taking apart the record or

> *trying to work around the binding to locate a certain form. This minor change allowed one to flip through a thick record easily to locate a certain form. One staff person told me it reminded her of having power windows in her car for the first time: how she rejoiced in the effortlessness of opening and closing them whenever she felt like it, versus the reaching and straining for the old crank windows. We also decided to color code the most frequently used forms. This not only helps you find the forms easier in the record, it adds a little variety into all of the paper we deal with. It's just nicer to have some, yellow, pink and green cross your desk at times.*

> *I always intended to bring information handouts to families but in the rush of managing my caseload and getting to home visits on time, I just didn't find time to make copies of the handouts. My supervisor knew that we weren't making use of the handouts and asked how he could help. We found the solution in having our secretary make multiple copies of handouts and organizing them by topic area in a file drawer. Now that I can just reach in the drawer and grab a handful at a time, I have given them out constantly. It was such a little thing, but it made a big difference. The nagging guilt that I wasn't doing the job the way I thought it should be done is gone, and my supervisor doesn't have to keep reminding me that I should be giving them out.*

Having support staff do as much of the busy work as possible—creating files, filling in basic information on forms, and so forth—can really free up the staff time and energy to focus on families. Have blank copies of forms neatly organized and accessible in either a file cabinet or forms holder.

> *Our administrative assistant now tracks all of the cases, compiles the new case record with basic forms, and has a computerized system that fills in family name and demographic information on progress note forms. The staff are incredibly appreciative of this "paperwork support" and their productivity shows it.*

Communicate Management Decisions

Top managers can set a positive tone for the workplace by having a regular flow of information to staff through meetings, e-mails, memos, and so forth. This communicates much more than information; it sets a tone that upper management cares about staff enough to include them and connect with them. Leaving staff in the dark about decisions until the last minute, or never providing the reasoning behind a major decision, creates an atmosphere of distrust and resentment among staff. Staff can swallow many bitter pills regarding cutbacks or reorganizations if they are kept in the loop and feel that, at least, management respected and care about them enough to come to them honestly and explain why it was necessary.

Help Staff Feel Safe in the Field

Safety is usually a concern for staff traveling into high crime areas and volatile family situations. Make sure staff have received training from a law enforcement or security professional on staying safe. Have staff travel in teams when needed, and go out with the staff person yourself, if she expresses significant concerns about visiting a particular family. Imagine the bonding experience it was for a staff person and supervisor who were cornered together in a mother's apartment when her estranged husband brought his attack dog to her home and had it standing and barking outside the door.

Create a Nurturing Environment: Little Things Mean a Lot

There may not be not a great deal that you as a supervisor can do to improve physical working conditions for your supervisees. Little things can mean a lot, however, especially if your staff see that you are concerned about their well-being. For example, get input from staff regarding physical office layout; accommodating how they prefer their desks be set up costs nothing. Put up a bulletin board with positive items about staff and agency accomplishments. This is likely to be more meaningful than generic posters with inspirational messages. Make sure the office is kept neat. Do not allow supplies and boxes to accumulate. Supply areas should be kept well stocked and neatly organized.

In one agency, the CEO forbade the purchase of "sticky notes" because he thought they were too expensive. One supervisor endeared herself to her staff forever by personally purchasing some for them. It was almost like forbidden fruit and all the sweeter to use because of it.

We have said this before, but it bears repeating because we have found it to be a powerful supervisory action: Providing food at meetings is always a good idea. Food makes people feel nurtured and, when staff feel they receive good things from their organizations, they often feel motivated to reciprocate the positive energy.

When staff spend a large percentage of their time in people's homes, their working conditions are clearly out of your control. But still there are ways to have an effect. One supervisor gave nice pens to her staff (purchased with her own money), and a supervisee expressed her appreciation: "When you're in a dirty house with a hostile, chaotic family, at least you feel good about writing with a nice pen." In a way, that pen symbolized the supervisor's support and caring for her staff and traveled with the staff person out into the community. These small symbols of the supervisor's caring probably helped that staff person to be more caring with the families she served.

Another suggestion here would be for supervisors to encourage caseworkers to do what they can to make their work areas pleasant and comfortable by, for instance, personalizing these areas with posters, photographs, and so forth.

Factor 5: Professional Self-Esteem

The next factor is called professional self-esteem. This is a simple factor with items that essentially ask participants about their evaluation of their work, confidence in their skills, and professional respect from colleagues. Professional self-esteem is indicated by agreeing with items such as, "I am confident in my ability to effectively serve my clients." It is indicated by disagreeing with items such as, "I sometimes wonder whether I really know what I am doing in my work."

Implications for Supervisors

For professionals, just as for clients, self-esteem has a component of reality and a component of perception. Effective supervisors help with both components by working to increase staff's level of competence and by directing their attention to the successes they achieve.

Give Challenging Work Assignments

It may not be possible to pick and choose the cases or tasks that you assign to your staff, given the demands of your workplace. Whenever it is possible, however, assess each of your staff's capabilities and deliberately assign cases you know will stretch their abilities. This communicates your confidence in the staff person while providing an opportunity for growth. As the worker succeeds in successively more difficult situations, a realistic sense of accomplishment and growth will enhance professional self-esteem.

Have Staff Develop a Specialty

Being recognized either in or outside the agency as a specialist in a certain area (sex abuse, domestic violence, work with preschoolers, etc.) can greatly enhance professional self-esteem and provide a focus for the staff member's learning goals. This recognition enhances agency resources and provides role models to other staff on avenues for professional growth.

Develop Best Practice Guidelines for Staff

Nothing increases self-esteem like success, so anything you do to strengthen your supervisees' job performance should have positive effects on their professional self-esteem. Your responsibility as a supervisor is to know what the state of the art is and then do all you can to have your staff follow these best practice guidelines. Professionals who believe they know what is available in the literature on best practices have more confidence that they are doing things right. Providing workers with effective tools gives them their best chance of having the experiences of success that contribute to a sense of personal efficacy and pride.

Give Supervisees Positive Feedback for Work Well Done

Our work in parenting programs shows that it is easy for parents to fall into the pattern of ignoring positive child behavior and focusing negative attention on inappropriate behavior. Although understandable, this is not an effective way to teach and encourage positive behavior! Unfortunately, it is just as easy for supervisors to fall into this pattern, because problems naturally attract more attention than successful work does. Nonetheless, supervisees learn as much from specific compliments that tell them what they have done right as they do from critical feedback that identifies areas for improvement. Positive feedback is a way for supervisors to enhance caseworkers' professional self-esteem, which is a component of job satisfaction.

Use of Realistic Standards of Evaluation

Research on depression and self-esteem highlights the important role of standards for evaluating performance. If standards are too low, people do not put forth much effort and do not perform well; they are too easy on themselves. If standards are too high, however, even people who try hard and perform satisfactorily see themselves as having failed.

Unrealistically high evaluative standards are one cause of depression and low self-esteem. The most effective evaluative standards are moderately high—not too high and not too low. This is equally true for self-evaluation and evaluation of other people. Supervisors can enhance their effectiveness by using moderate, realistic criteria in providing feedback to supervisees. In human services work, moderate standards involve realistic aspirations for improvement in client functioning; supervisors should consider significant progress a success, even if serious problems remain. Such standards can encourage improving levels of performance and bolster caseworkers' professional self-esteem, which will enhance their satisfaction with work. Supervisees who feel competent will feel better about their jobs and perform more effectively. Accurate and positive feedback will brighten anyone's day!

Factor 6: Futility and Avoidance

The last factor is futility and avoidance. The items in this factor ask participants to agree or disagree with descriptions of a sense of helplessness and apathy at work. The co-occurrence of futility and avoidance in one factor is not surprising; the two elements are logically connected. A sense of futility may lead to avoidance, because people come to believe that efforts do not produce benefits. Work then becomes dreary and frustrating, and professionals begin to avoid work. An example of the futility component of this factor is, "I sometimes feel there is nothing I can do to help my clients." An instance of the avoidance component is, "I sometimes call in sick because I just need a break from work."

The futility and avoidance factor corresponds closely to the term *burnout*. The specific experiences depicted by the items suggest a history of discouraging experiences that overwhelm the individual's capacity to cope. Feeling helpless and hopeless, these professionals, not illogically, sometimes respond by giving up, because trying does not seem to make any difference.

Managers can intervene to reduce this aspect of burnout on several levels, with the most appropriate intervention depending on the supervisee's specific difficulty. Like low self-esteem, a sense of futility can be based either on a genuine lack of effective work skills or on an inaccurate assessment of the effectiveness of one's work with clients.

Implications for Supervisors

Teach Skills that Effectively Benefit Clients

The solution to weak professional skills is generally additional training, assuming the supervisee is capable of doing the job. If the worker's skills are adequate, an appropriate strategy would be to increase the supervisee's awareness of the likely effect of those skills. The level of aspiration is relevant here: If, for instance, the worker's goal is to dramatically transform a parent's functioning overnight, he or she will probably miss the smaller but important positive effects that the intervention achieves.

Point Out Positive Effects on Clients

Supervisors can point out to caseworkers that even if an allegation was not substantiated, the investigation itself may have had some positive effects. The abusers may have been left with some sense that their behavior could really get them in trouble or harm the child. As another example, supervisors can point out that the failure of a reunification attempt does not mean the services did not benefit the parent. Services may have provided something positive that can be built on by future services until the parent achieves an adequate level of child-rearing capability or at least becomes able to play a positive part in the child's life, even if placement elsewhere is necessary.

Emphasize the Importance of the Work Even When Setbacks Occur

The component of avoidance can generally be addressed with interventions for the futility aspect of this factor; most professionals will re-engage in work when they have the sense that their efforts make a difference. To help with this, supervisors can emphasize the importance of caseworkers' efforts, particularly at times when setbacks cause workers to doubt the importance of these efforts. The severe problems of some clients can make work with them seem discouraging, but these problems also make this work vitally important.

Research on depression shows that when people underestimate the intrinsic or inherent difficulty of tasks, they undervalue their performance on those tasks. In other words, to cope effectively with difficult work, it is important to realize how difficult that work is. Human services professionals have a special and demanding role in our society: working with people experiencing severe problems, dysfunction, and pain. Great value is found in this work because if it were not done, the most vulnerable members of our community would be left to even worse suffering. But one inevitable characteristic of this work is that success is hard to achieve and disappointments are inescapable. Understanding this clearly will help providers value the increments of success they do achieve and give themselves deserved credit for being involved in this vital endeavor.

Conclusion

Job satisfaction is a multifaceted concept of six main factors. In our research sample, although sense of attained personal competence was significant, job satisfaction was more dependent on perceived opportunities to further develop professional skills. The two most important factors, self-actualization and achievement support, both include items that show learning and developing skills as a continuing process. In contrast, the professional self-esteem factor, which has items illustrating the respondent's attained level of skill, was fifth in importance.

Thus, respondents' orientations were more dynamic than static, with more focus on where they were going than on where they were. Workers were more concerned with environmental support for continuing skill development than with recognition of their existing levels of achievement. The findings suggest it is more important to create a work environment that supports continuing development of competencies than to compliment professionals on their achieved quality of performance.

Part 2

Strategies to Prevent Burnout in Your Staff

Chapter 4 | Variables that Affect Job Satisfaction and Burnout

Once we examined what makes up job satisfaction, the next obvious question was, "What variables affect job satisfaction and burnout?" In other words, why do some people burn out quickly, whereas others maintain high job satisfaction for years? We looked at a number of factors that might affect job satisfaction, including characteristics of the individual and work environment. This chapter describes the surprising results, along with their implications for supervisors.

Demographics: "You Can't Tell a Burned-Out Worker by Her Cover"

Demographic variables proved to be poor predictors of job satisfaction. No difference existed between males and females in job satisfaction. Nonwhite participants expressed the same levels of satisfaction with their work as white participants. To examine the relationship between job satisfaction and education level, the researchers grouped the data for academic degrees into three levels: bachelor's degree (bachelors' of arts, science, and social work), master's degree (masters' of arts, science, social work, and education), and doctoral degrees (PhD, PsyD, MD, JD). Job satisfaction was not related to the participants' academic training.

Job Characteristics

Salary showed a correlation with work satisfaction that was statistically significant, but quite low in magnitude. It is interesting that in casual conversation, people often attribute more importance to salary as a factor in job satisfaction than what research studies usually find. A low correlation between satisfaction and salary in the human service field is not very surprising, however, because people for whom money is a strong motivating factor would not choose to work in this field. In our profession, more altruistic motives are at work.

Job satisfaction scores were significantly different for full-time and part-time workers, with part-time workers expressing higher satisfaction. This difference may be explained simply because part-time work involves less stress and less likelihood that professionals will become tired of repetitious aspects of their work. Although this finding seems to strengthen the case for part-time work arrangements, managers must balance this consideration against practical job requirements, and workers must balance it against their financial needs. The number of vacation days workers earned was not related to job satisfaction.

Years of Experience

Years in human service work showed a small positive correlation with satisfaction. Age, which was closely related to years of experience, showed a similar correlation. Thus, older, more experienced professionals were happier with their work. An association between time in an occupation and satisfaction with one's work is a finding that has been replicated across a variety of occupations. The usual explanation is based on a process of self-selection: Workers who are unhappy in their jobs tend to leave the field, so that, over time, remaining workers are likely to be satisfied with their jobs. Nonetheless, this finding is encouraging in its implication that spending time in human services work does not necessarily lead to burnout.

Educational Activity

The number of professional articles and books that participants reported reading in the past year showed a fairly strong correlation with satisfaction. Days of training in the past year were also positively related to satisfaction. Thus, workers who engaged in a lot of educational activities were happier in their jobs than those who did little reading and training. This is an interesting finding, given that the individual's level of education was not correlated with job satisfaction. Thus, work satisfaction is related to learning while on the job, not the amount of education received in school.

These correlational results cannot determine whether educational activity increases job satisfaction or vice versa. Nonetheless, the desire for training and reading has a consistent pattern in the results. Factor analysis indicated that intellectual curiosity, stimulation, and absorption in work are important components of job satisfaction for people in the helping professions. For these individuals, job satisfaction seems to hinge largely on a sense that one's work involves learning, skill building, and exercising one's mind. If so, the educational activities of training and reading would contribute to a satisfying sense that work contributes to intellectual growth.

Workers' Own Victimization Histories

The questionnaire included a set of questions about the respondent's personal history of victimization. The study included these questions because it seemed possible that such histories might have affected participants' job satisfaction. Unexpectedly, we found that sexual abuse survivors obtained higher scores on the work satisfaction measure than professionals with no reported sexual abuse history. A personal history of child neglect was also associated with higher job satisfaction, although this finding is tentative because of the small number of participants reporting neglect. The study found no difference for childhood physical abuse. Adult experience of violent victimization was not related to job satisfaction, nor was whether respondents reported that their children had experienced maltreatment.

The findings for sexual abuse survivors should be interpreted cautiously. It should not be concluded that the typical survivor of child maltreatment would be likely to be highly satisfied in a job working with victims, because survivors who enter and remain in such occupations are a small, highly self-selected group within the population of adult survivors. For members of this group, who probably possess special characteristics, a history of maltreatment during childhood is not a liability but a potential asset. These professionals may be able to draw on memories and sensitivities originating in their childhoods to empathize more effectively with their clients, and the personal meaning of their work with victims may strengthen their involvement in their jobs.

Implications for Supervisors

Increasing Job Satisfaction Is an Attainable Goal

Gender, ethnic group, and academic degree seem to be of no value in predicting adaptation to human services work. These findings are encouraging in their implications for supervisors' ability to make a difference in staff's job experience, because those concrete variables are not controllable. In contrast, the results identified several potentially controllable variables that do affect work satisfaction.

Provide Part-Time and Flex-Time Work Arrangements

Administrators should consider the feasibility of part-time work arrangements. Although practical obstacles are sometimes present and the necessary arrangements would vary from setting to setting, results indicate that the availability of part-time positions for staff who want them would probably reduce burnout, work avoidance, and job turnover. These positive effects would benefit organizations and clients as well as workers themselves.

Encourage Reading and Training

The results suggest that increasing opportunities for work-related intellectual development increases the job satisfaction of human service professionals. Managers could provide such opportunities by allowing time for training and reading either independently or, perhaps even more effective, as part of group activities involving social interaction as a mode of continuing educational development. Case conferences and teamwork on cases would provide another context for the exchange of ideas and mutual teaching and learning.

Managers must face the practical consideration that such procedures take time. Gains in expertise, enthusiasm for work, motivation, job satisfaction, and commitment to the field, however, would likely be benefits of these activities, and resulting gains in productivity might more than compensate for the time invested in professional skill development.

Set up opportunities for reading professional books and articles. This can be done by via a small library in the office—just a bookshelf with some well-chosen classics and current issues of, for example, *Child Welfare; Social Work; The International Journal of Child Abuse and Neglect; Psychotherapy:*

Theory, Research, and Practice; and *Psychotherapy Networker.* Ask your staff what books or journals they think would help them in their work. Invite staff to let each other know what they are reading and to make recommendations for the team. You can copy and distribute articles that they strongly recommend with a note identifying the staff member making the recommendation.

On a smaller scale, encourage reading by circulating articles of interest to your supervisees. Provide new staff with a binder filled with some articles you consider classics, so that right from the start, they get the idea that this agency is a place where learning and growth are part of the program.

Obviously, to create a learning environment, you, too, will need to be active in learning. Set aside at least 30 minutes a week to read an article or go to an Internet site to keep up with current practice. Try to close your door and avoid answering the phone during this time. Being a role model is key to the supervisory relationship. Staying abreast of the field is just as important as pushing the paper that comes across your desk and has the added bonus of helping prevent your own burnout.

Create Agency Policies that Support Learning

Make at least one learning goal part of each person's job responsibilities at their annual evaluation. Have the staff member identify any topic they would like to know more about and develop a realistic goal (e.g., reading two articles, doing an Internet search) as part of their performance evaluation. A learning goal could be, "Understand the effects of witnessing domestic violence on a preschooler," or "Learn techniques to support a recovering substance abuser in sobriety."

Provide an allotment of training days and training dollars to each person to be used with the approval of their supervisor. Giving staff both time and money to pursue training sends a powerful message about the agency's commitment to their growth and learning.

Encourage Big Picture Thinking

Supervisors are in a good position to contribute to the educational and intellectual stimulation their supervisees experience at work. Although it is easy to get bogged down in the process of trying to get all the work done, devoting some time and energy to stepping back and thinking about the conceptual issues involved in tasks and decisions seems to add a positive dimension to work experience. Job satisfaction can be enhanced by supervision that goes beyond the routine aspects of work and involves an intellectually substantial attempt to understand the causes and consequences of client problems and the ways that interventions can help. It can be rewarding to bring up a book or article that addresses issues involved in a case and to suggest the supervisee take a look at it. New ideas, interesting information, and insightful analysis may not only make supervision more enjoyable but may also enliven the overall job experience.

Helping Workers with Victimization Histories

The findings regarding sexual abuse survivors do not seem to have any direct implications for supervisors beyond indicating that a worker's history of maltreatment is no automatic reason for concern. It might be useful to convey these findings to staff, in a group setting and with no identification of personal histories, because this information might be meaningful to professionals who do have an abuse history. These survivors should know that although their work might stimulate painful memories at times, they may be able to integrate their past unfortunate experiences into a meaningful work endeavor that will bring benefits to clients facing similar challenges.

Chapter 5 | Coping Style

Although all jobs contain some stress, given the serious stressors associated with work in the helping professions, we believed that workers' coping styles might be especially important to their job experiences—and that is what the results indicated. We found that the coping mechanisms participants reported using in response to stressors at work showed important relations to their levels of job satisfaction. The study measured coping style with an adaptation of the Ways of Coping Questionnaire (Folkman & Lazarus, 1988). We modified the directions to this instrument by asking participants to respond to items in terms of a stressful experience they had experienced at work.*

Three coping styles were associated with high levels of job satisfaction. Participants who reported using these styles in response to stressors at work also expressed relatively high levels of job satisfaction:

- planful problem solving,
- positive reappraisal, and
- seeking social support.

The study also found that three coping mechanisms were associated with low levels of job satisfaction. Professionals who reported using these strategies to cope with stressors at work also expressed relatively low levels of job satisfaction. The three coping styles associated with burnout were:

---

* All items in this chapter are reproduced by special permission of the publisher, Mindgarden, Inc., 1690 Woodside Rd., Suite 202, Redwood City, CA 94061, USA, www.mindgarden.com, from the *Ways of Coping* by Susan Folkman and Richard Lazarus, © 1988 by Consulting Psychologists Press. All rights reserved. Further reproduction is prohibited without the publisher's written consent.

- confrontive coping,
- escape and avoidance, and
- accepting responsibility.

These coping mechanisms are described in the following sections, including questionnaire items that describe the specific psychological processes involved in the category of coping response. The individual items are worth examining because they describe the particular psychological operations that together make up a style of coping.

Adaptive Coping Strategies

Planful problem solving involves thinking through the stressful situation, putting together a plan, and then doing something to address the source of stress; it is a combination of thought and action. Planful problem solving was the coping mechanism with the strongest relationship to job satisfaction. Examples of these items are:

- I made a plan of action and followed it.
- Just concentrated on what I had to do next—the next step.
- Came up with a couple of different solutions to the problem.

Positive reappraisal means coping by searching for some positive result of the stressor, such as personal growth, improved priorities, or increased faith. This is an inwardly oriented coping style. It has a philosophical quality, and a broad perspective to these coping responses exists:

- I came out of the experience better than when I went in.
- I rediscovered what is important in life.
- I changed something about myself.

Seeking social support means going to other people for advice, concrete help, or comfort. This is an externally oriented coping approach involving transactions with the interpersonal world:

- I talked to someone who could do something concrete about the problem.
- I talked to someone about how I was feeling.
- I got professional help.

Maladaptive Coping Strategies

Confrontive coping involves taking some direct action in response to the stressor. Several of these items include an element of emotionality, and the items do not depict much thought prior to the overt response:

- I stood my ground and fought for what I wanted.
- I let my feelings out somehow.
- I did something I didn't think would work, but at least I was doing something.

Escape and avoidance involves hoping for or fantasizing about some dramatic resolution to the problem and trying to soothe oneself using distractions such as food, sleep, or drugs. These process have a passive quality and an absence of effort to meaningfully address the problem:

- I had fantasies or wishes about how things might turn out.
- I tried to make myself feel better by eating, drinking, smoking, using drugs or medication, etc.
- I took it out on other people.

Accepting responsibility refers to coping mechanisms that include some acknowledgement that one was personally responsible for the stressful event. These items are more than simply accepting responsibility—they have a quality of self-blame, guilt and self-punishment:

- I criticized or lectured myself.
- I apologized or did something to make up.

Implications for Supervisors

Inform Your Staff

The first way for supervisors to make use of these findings is simply by informing supervisees about them. This is a case in which knowledge can lead directly to benefit. Workers are potentially in control of the strategies with which they respond to stress, and knowing which coping mechanisms are effective and which are ineffective can lead people to use the more helpful strategies.

Model and Encourage Effective Coping Strategies

Supervisors can make active use of the strategies by structuring the discussion of stressful cases in ways that encourage effective coping processes. Establishing some shared vocabulary and knowledge about effective and ineffective coping would facilitate this process, but it is not essential to use the terminology presented here. The important supervisory task is to recognize when staff are using coping responses that are making their stress experiences worse and then to model and encourage use of more effective strategies.

Effective supervisor responses to stressed staff members must be individualized to the specifics of each situation, but a formula can give a helpful response. When you perceive a supervisee to be angrily confronting a stressful situation, avoiding engagement with the problem, or blaming themselves for the upsetting situation, suggest that they switch their focus either to developing a plan for addressing the problem, finding some hopeful or consoling aspect of the situation, or seeking help from others.

One important pitfall to avoid is expressing a glib view of the stressor that invalidates the supervisee's experience. Because of the serious pain and danger involved in some cases, if you seem to dismiss your staff member's concern, you will probably be perceived as unsympathetic and not understanding. Your message should not be, "Oh, don't worry too much, it will probably work out somehow," because, unfortunately, that is not always true. Nonetheless, effective coping means that workers are not crushed into a hopeless, burned-out state by the stressors they face. The task is to achieve a balance between realistic acknowledgment of the stressor and resilient optimism.

Comparing helpful and maladaptive coping mechanisms reveals some general themes. Both planful problem solving and positive reappraisal involve a certain type of balance between components that is present in a more extreme form in the ineffective coping techniques. This is a balance between a hopeful interpretation of the situation and realistic perception of the stressor. In planful problem solving, the worker acknowledges the difficulty, but does not view the situation as unchangeable, and takes steps to address it. In positive reappraisal, the worker views the situation as unchangeable, but attempts to respond positively to the setback by making constructive changes in himself or herself.

The ineffective coping mechanisms generally do not share this balance between optimism and pessimism, but tend to fall at one extreme or the other. The escape and avoidance responses lack realistic acknowledgement of the stressor, as the person either fantasizes about perfect, magical solutions or withdraws attention from the problem. The responses in the accepting responsibility factor go to the opposite extreme. Here, self-blame is predominant and optimism is absent, as the individual castigates herself for causing the problem. Overall, the pattern of results suggests that work is enhanced by coping responses involving a moderate, balanced combination of optimism and realistic pessimism, rather than an extreme of either ignoring the problem or deprecating oneself for having caused it.

The third helpful strategy, seeking support from other people, can bring several different kinds of help to an individual facing a difficult situation. Other people can offer concrete aid in addressing the problem and can provide information or advice to enable the worker to resolve the situation and, failing that, can offer support and comfort to facilitate processing emotions in a positive manner.

Although the focus of this research was on professionals, the clients of human service agencies probably experience more stress than the staff, and they may be in need of help in developing effective coping responses. Thus, staff could use this information to help their clients cope more successfully with the stressors in their lives.

Reference

Folkman, S., & Lazarus, R. S. (1988). Coping as a mediator of emotion. *Journal of Personality and Social Psychology, 54*, 466–475.

Chapter 6: Thinking Patterns Associated with Job Satisfaction

Having examined how personal characteristics, job characteristics, and coping strategies affect job satisfaction, we now turn to the final area of interest: how people think. To study this, we constructed a questionnaire for measuring a variety of perceptions, thoughts, attitudes, and beliefs pertaining to work with child victims and other human service clients. We hypothesized that important relationships exist between work-related cognitions and job satisfaction, and the findings were in line with the hypotheses.

Attitudes Toward Learning

Participants high in job satisfaction tended to agree with the statement that professional trainings and reading are helpful to work. They tended to disagree with statements that the field has an inadequate knowledge base and that even the experts do not know how to help many clients. It appears that a devaluation of the field's knowledge is associated with burnout in providers, perhaps because this belief leaves them feeling that effective guidance for their work does not exist, which contributes to the futility aspect of burnout.

For highly satisfied respondents, a belief in their profession's expertise may enhance the work experience by providing a sense that answers to their difficulties with clients exist and by offering opportunities for intellectual stimulation and development through study. Satisfied human service workers believe that expert knowledge exists in the field, and they actively pursue it as they focus on becoming more expert themselves.

Balancing Work and Other Priorities

Two items pertained to participants' ability to mentally put aside thoughts about work during their free time. Highly satisfied workers tended to agree and burned-out participants to disagree with statements such as:

- I am able to leave my work behind at the end of the day if I want to, and I'm not troubled by job worries during my leisure time.
- I have leisure time activities (e.g., hobbies, friends, and interests) that really help me get my mind off work.

Thus, job experience seems to be enhanced by putting work aside at times, and involvement in other interests may leave professionals refreshed and energized when they return to work. The importance of nonwork involvement seems to extend to the area of self-esteem. Workers with burnout were likely to agree and satisfied participants to disagree with the statement, "My general self-esteem depends heavily on how successful I am with my clients."

This finding suggests that work experience is most positive for professionals whose lives and self-concepts do not depend too heavily on their work role. Workers with high job satisfaction seem to have a sense of balance between their professional and personal lives, and their concerns about work do not intrude into life outside the office. These professionals are not consumed by their job; instead, they keep their job in its place.

The Professional's Personal Issues

I can always tell when a family is really pushing my buttons. I'm very relieved when they don't show up for an appointment.

Given the emotionally charged work in which child welfare staff are engaged, it is inevitable that some families will evoke difficult personal reactions in workers. This should not be viewed by the staff person or the supervisor as a sign of weakness or a lack of expertise, but as an occupational hazard of human service work that can be managed if it is acknowledged and processed in supervision.

The questionnaire included three items that pertained to professionals' experiences of their own psychological issues in work with clients. The results for these items indicate that it is important for providers to

Thinking Patterns Associated with Job Satisfaction

have a degree of mastery of their own issues. High scores on the job satisfaction questionnaire were associated with disagreement with the following statements:

- I feel uncomfortable discussing sexual issues with my clients.
- At times, I feel my own personal emotional issues make my job more upsetting and difficult for me.
- My own sexual issues sometimes make things more difficult for me in my work with clients.

It is not surprising that the existence of unresolved personal conflicts and emotional concerns, particularly about sexuality, are associated with low satisfaction and increased likelihood of burnout in human service professionals who work with abused children. It is important to remember that whether workers have experienced trauma themselves is not the key, because people with a history of abuse actually had high job satisfaction. The important thing is whether workers have unresolved personal issues, whatever their source.

Although every worker will have difficulty working with some families, for most of your staff, this will be a small portion of their caseload. If the worker's personal issues pervade their entire work experience, then personal therapy is the most appropriate course of action. Depending on the worker's ability to be effective during the therapy process, she may also need to move into a different role in the agency or outside of it until personal issues are more manageable.

Sometimes personal issues affect worker effectiveness in subtle ways. For example, a worker avoids bringing up a specific issue with a parent, although she is aware that it needs to be discussed. The supervisor needs to identify this for the worker, because she is probably avoiding the issue in supervision as well. Of course, this will make it hard to see the issue in supervision, but indications of this type of problem may be apparent when you have a sense of a piece being missing in a supervisee's description of a difficult case.

As a supervisor, it is crucial for you to let your staff know that when they encounter a family that upsets them, they should bring that issue to you, so that you can discuss it in supervision. Recognizing one's own reaction to a family and the effects of that reaction on one's effectiveness is an important growth experience for a human service professional. Talking it through in supervision, even recognizing that this invisible obstacle exists, will help. Staff should know that, if needed, you will assign the case to another worker—although they should also be aware that this can only be a rare occurrence. Still, knowing that an escape exists may allow the worker to continue with the family and become more effective, instead of feeling trapped and resentful.

> *I felt so angry at how this mother was treating her young son that I wanted to walk across the room and scream at her. This adorable 3-year-old ran to her smiling to show her a picture he had drawn, and she just ignored him, turning away and lighting a cigarette. I walked into supervision this week and told my boss that I wasn't going back into that house—I couldn't stand to see that mother reject that little boy one more time. My supervisor sat and really listened to me for the first time, and told me that she finally understood how upsetting this was for me, and that I didn't have to continue to work with this family. Somehow, once she said that, I knew that I could go back. And I did. On the very next visit, I realized that I had engaged the mother in a way I had never been able to before, because for the first time I was truly trying to take her perspective. I think it's because my supervisor understood and empathized with me that I could turn around and empathize with that mother.*

Optimism and Pessimism in Work with Clients

The questionnaire also included a number of items that concerned optimism versus pessimism, difficulty versus ease, and success versus failure in work with clients. Some of the items pertained to client progress or its lack, and some referred to the worker's internal experience of service provision. The pattern of correlations between these items and scores on the job satisfaction measure was extremely consistent, suggesting an important pattern of results.

Two of the items made statements related to work with clients that were optimistic in a simple, straightforward way. No correlation existed between job satisfaction and responses to these items:

- People are never subjected to misfortunes that they do not have the capability to endure.
- I feel that I should be able to significantly help all my clients.

Three items made simply pessimistic statements about the intrinsic capability of services to help clients (as distinct from respondents' personal competence). No correlation existed between job satisfaction and responses to these items:

- No matter what the quality of my work with my clients, the fact is that the overall quality of their lives is mostly beyond my control.
- There are some clients whose problems are so severe that even the most skillful and dedicated work with them will not produce much benefit.
- The work I do is difficult for most of the people who do it.

These nonsignificant results raise a puzzling question: If neither optimism nor pessimism is related to job satisfaction and burnout, what type of thinking does make a difference?

Combining Hope and Realism

In contrast to the five items whose statements about the difficulty of work with clients were simply either optimistic or pessimistic, seven statements combined positive and negative features. These statements combined their optimistic and pessimistic elements in a certain, distinctive way. An acknowledgement of the difficulty or even the limited possibilities of work was combined with a hopeful statement about valuable gains that could be made in the context of these limitations.

Significant correlations existed between job satisfaction and agreement with all seven of these two-part statements combining elements of pessimism and optimism. Satisfied participants were likely to agree and workers with burnout to disagree with the following statements:

- Even when a child's future appears to be dismal, their future can include dramatically positive changes.
- Although some clients may never be able to function really well, effective services can be of some benefit to even the most impaired clients.
- I do not expect myself to resolve all of my clients' difficulties, and I am content if I have a significant positive effect, even if many problems remain.

- If I feel I am on the right track with a client, it doesn't bother me if progress is slow.

- Even when a client appears to make no progress, I can appreciate the learning I gain from my work with that person.

- Even when my clients do not seem to benefit from my work with them, it is possible that they have received something positive that just hasn't become visible.

- I focus my concern on those aspects of my clients' lives I can positively influence, and I don't take responsibility for the many factors beyond my control.

Acknowledging the Negative and Appreciating the Positive

Some of the items are about expectations for future change, and others are about attitudes toward the results of work that has already been done. The principle underlying both types of items is that the existence of the negative does not negate the positive; instead, they combine an awareness of both. With regard to current situations, this means the worker both acknowledges sad realities and appreciates what progress has occurred.

Consider an example of a family that began treatment in a state of serious dysfunction, with a mother addicted to cocaine who sometimes physically abused her child. That child's aggressive behavior had resulted in his suspension from school. At the end of treatment, the mother's drug use seemed reduced but was definitely not eliminated; she was trying to replace corporal punishment with a reinforcement system, but still sometimes engaged in seriously inappropriate parenting behaviors. The child's placement in a special education class had brought his behavior under some control, although he was still several years behind grade level and often got in fights after school. Both mother and child still seemed to be emotionally damaged individuals, and it was difficult to envision them living a life that child welfare workers would find satisfactory. Nonetheless, the mother has apologized to the child for the abuse and has learned some effective child management techniques. When the child experiences feelings of rage, he now uses an anger management technique that sometimes seems to prevent an explosion of violence. The case has been terminated; there will be no further services.

Our question concerns the worker's personal evaluation of a case like this. There are two main possibilities. Some workers look at a family situation like this and feel that the dysfunction and misery have barely been dented and will probably return completely a few months after termination; they expect the drug use, physical abuse, and child behavior problems to recur and, even if they do not, the life they envision for the family seems tragically limited, painful, and disappointing.

Other professionals look at the same situation and have a cautious sense of hope along with a modest appreciation of the gains that have been made in the context of severe dysfunction. They recognize that several forms of relapse might take the family back to their previous intolerable situation, but they also think that the mother might be able to keep her cocaine use under some control, her improved child management skills might put the child on a better developmental course, his special education program might allow him to get something out of school, and the occasional laughs and rough kindnesses shared by the two are enough to make life worth living in their family. Such professionals notice, in the midst of the family's mostly dysfunctional interactions, occasional bits of newly learned, more effective behavior that clearly came from services provided to the family.

Neither professional is more logical or rational than the other. The difference between these two views is not a difference of accuracy or correctness, because no objective answer to the question of whether the family's gains really matter exists, given the deficits that remain. But our findings indicate this: The two views will have very different implications for work experience, with one leading to burnout and the other to high job satisfaction.

The same glass can be viewed as half full and as half empty. In our work, many glasses are one-tenth full and nine-tenths empty. Regardless, however, our experience of situations in which positive and negative features combine is largely a function of where we focus and what we emphasize in our thoughts. The family has improved somewhat, and yet they are far from being happy and truly functional. Is this good enough?

Professionals who are happy in human service work tend to feel that it is. These workers seem to focus more on the effects of their interventions than on the client's overall level of well-being, which is a function of factors beyond the professional's control. It is the difference between being happy about seeing some improvement versus being unhappy that the workers did not bring about a cure. Intervention can move clients only within the limits imposed by the basic frameworks of their life situations, but job satisfaction seems to be enhanced by an emphasis on movement occurring within this constraint.

Based on our results, we can reconstruct the thoughts of the typical resilient, satisfied professional as going something like this:

> *They still have a lot of problems, but they were worse off when they came to me, and they are better off now because of our work together; we accomplished something. There's nothing I could have done about the awful situation that was their starting point, and I'm glad I was able to move them forward from there.*

Implications for Supervisors

Teach Supervisees the Alcoholics Anonymous Serenity Prayer

One theme running through many of these items is a differentiation between problems the worker can change and those he or she cannot ameliorate. This issue is clearly delineated by the Serenity Prayer often cited by Alcoholics Anonymous:

> *God grant me the serenity to accept the things I cannot change, the courage to change the things I can, and the wisdom to know the difference.*

The significance of this prayer for us does not lie in its religious content, but in the way its understanding of problems points toward adaptive emotional responses, especially with regard to what it says about personal control. Both overestimation and underestimation of the potential effects of our work impairs work satisfaction and job performance. Service providers who feel they have no control over any aspect of their clients' situations experience a sense of futility that causes withdrawal from involvement in work and deprives clients of the help the workers could offer. Professionals who overestimate their control over clients' situations set themselves up for inevitable disappointments, which will accumulate to produce burnout. Supervisors are in a strong position to help staff with the complex intellectual task of differentiating factors that they can and cannot control. Emotional energy should be focused on controllable factors.

Discourage Unrealistic Hopelessness About Clients' Potential for Change

It can be useful for professionals to reflect that because their work purposefully seeks out human suffering, their sense of the world includes a greater preponderance of suffering than exists in general. Helping professionals go to where the trouble is, and to maintain their resilience, they need to remember that theirs is a troubled portion of the world; moving this portion forward, even if only a little, is a valuable mission in the community.

Denial of the sad and tragic is maladaptive, however, acknowledgment of sad realities followed by appreciation of the value of positive elements in the same situation is not denial. The capability to function comfortably and effectively in the midst of human suffering seems to depend largely on this combination of acknowledging the negative and appreciating the positive.

Help Caseworkers Evaluate Client Progress from Their Starting Point

Workers whose thinking follows the form of the two-part items in the study are able to meet clients where they are. They can respond to even highly disturbed or suffering clients with acceptance and without extreme discouragement, and they can go on to the task of moving the client forward.

These workers can gauge progress in terms of the client's starting point, not in terms of an abstract standard of how well people should be able to function. Such providers set goals that realistically acknowledge both the potential for progress and constraints on positive change. Their evaluation of work is realistic but not lax. In contrast, a simple optimism about work with clients provides only brittle protection against the frustrating outcomes that inevitably occur with clients at times. Although a general sense that life is good and people can solve all their own problems might seem helpful in principle, this type of optimism would not long survive the stressors of human service work. Only optimism that is leavened with realism can survive exposure to negative outcomes. In other words, purely optimistic expectancies are disconfirmed by negative outcomes, leaving the professional demoralized, whereas expectancies combining positive and negative elements can accommodate both good and bad outcomes.

Discourage Unrealistic Hopes for Dramatic Resolution of Client Difficulties

Supervisors should discuss realistic levels of aspiration with their caseworkers. Supervisors can share the idea that some factors that have hurtful or limiting effects on clients are beyond the worker's control, but within these boundaries, workers have the opportunity to facilitate important change. The key message is that limitations to progress do not negate the value of the progress that does occur. It is worthwhile to help clients even if we do not "save" or "cure" them. It is possible to acknowledge the negative while focusing on the positive. Realism and optimism can be integrated.

People with these mixed expectancies are in a position to respond to negative situations with a determination to work toward progress from that starting point. Integration of positive and negative realities can enable hope to coexist with acknowledgement of tragedy in life. A cognitive process of this type is an effective means of coping with job-related stress and protects against burnout when work is difficult and setbacks occur.

Chapter 7: A Review and Challenge

Jessica Job Satisfaction: A Review

So now we understand why Jessica bounds into work on Monday morning. She feels that she is growing professionally and that this growth is supported by her workplace and supervisor. She is realistic but hopeful in her approach to the difficult families with whom she works. When troubles arise on the job, she has effective coping strategies to manage them. Whatever personal issues she may have had, she has resolved them so they do not interfere with her effectiveness on the job. She has balanced priorities, so that her job does not intrude on her personal life. She acknowledges the unchangeable, negative realities of her clients' lives, but, nonetheless, she values the gains they make. Jessica is resilient, which means that experiences with the tragic, painful realities of the world do not damage her; she integrates these experiences into a positive adaptation to life.

Taking Care of Yourself: A Final Note

Since you have survived the system long enough to have been promoted to the supervisory level, you appear to have avoided burnout as a line worker. You are now presented with new stresses as a supervisor. We believe the suggestions offered here apply to you as well, however, some additional strategies that a supervisor can use to protect her own ability to function effectively in her role exist.

Set Reasonable Boundaries on Your Accessibility

Having an open-door policy and being very accessible to your staff may have a positive effect on their work life, but you must be careful not to sacrifice yourself in the process. You should shut your door and protect some time each day to catch up on tasks, file away papers, and keep your office in order. This would also be the time to read a journal article or stay abreast of professional developments in the field via the Internet, newsletters, and so forth. Staff will not resent this if you explain that you use your closed-door periods during the day to do some of the self-care, coping, and time management strategies that you also recommend to them. Just as we advise parents to take a time-out when their stress level becomes high, you may need to separate from staff for a period of time simply to have some time by yourself. If you get burned out, you will not be able to help your staff prevent their own burnout.

Meet with Other Supervisors for Support

As good as your relationship may be with your staff, there are certain things you will not be able to discuss with them and certain boundaries that you cannot cross because of your position as their supervisor. Also, you probably experience some stressors that only another supervisor would truly understand. That is why it is important for you to cultivate relationships with peers in your organization: You, too, need and deserve a shoulder to cry on and an ear to listen to you. Meeting as an organized group and developing one-on-one relationships are both helpful.

Have a Sense of Humor

Although we did not attempt to measure sense of humor in our study, we believe that it may be an additional feature of the coping of people who are able to avoid burnout. Although we face so many tough situations that have little humor in them, humorous aspects certainly exist in the work we do, and we need to see them and appreciate them.

Remember the earlier story about the supervisor and her staff person trapped in a family's home because the violent, estranged husband had placed an attack dog outside the door? That supervisor returned to the office and managed to inject some humor into the story, describing how they were throwing the hot dogs from the family's lunch to the dog to mollify him. She talked about how ironic it was that the point of the trip was to deliver a cell phone to the mother so she could call police if needed, only to discover that when she tried to use that cell phone to call for help, the battery was dead. She had managed to transform a very frightening situation into a ridiculous one, and we all laughed about it.

The Challenge Ahead

You probably have at least one Barbara Burnout on your staff right now, or someone well on their way to burnout. Here is our challenge. Instead of dreading your next supervision time with her, figure out which ideas you will use try to help her recover from her burnout. Can you succeed in helping her become more satisfied and productive? Imagine your level of job satisfaction if you succeed!

SUGGESTIONS FOR FURTHER READING

Fenichel, E. (Ed.). (1992). *Learning through supervision and mentorship to support the development of infants, toddlers, and their families: A source book.* Washington, DC: Zero to Three.

Folkman, S., & Lazarus, R. S. (1988). Coping as a mediator of emotion. *Journal of Personality and Social Psychology, 54*, 466–475.

Freudenberger, H. J. (1975). Staff burnout. *Journal of Social Issues, 30*, 159–165.

Fryer, G. E., Miyoshi, T. J., & Thomas, P. J. (1989). The relationship of child protection worker attitudes to attrition from the field. *Child Abuse & Neglect, 13*, 345–350.

Koeske, G. F., Kirk, S. A., & Koeske, R. D. (1993). Coping with job stress: Which strategies work best? *Journal of Occupational and Organizational Psychology, 66*, 319–335.

Kottler, J. A. (1993). *On being a therapist.* San Francisco: Jossey-Bass.

Maslach, C. (1982). *Burnout: The cost of caring.* New York: Prentice-Hall.

McCann, L., & Pearlman, L. A. (1990). Vicarious traumatization: A framework for understanding the psychological effects of working with victims. *Journal of Traumatic Stress, 3*, 131–147.

Morton, T. D., & Salus, M. K. (1994) *Supervising child protective services caseworkers.* Washington, DC: U.S. Department of Health and Human Services.

Raquepay, J. M., & Miller, R. S. (1989). Psychotherapist burnout: A componential analysis. *Professional Psychology: Research and Practice, 20*, 32–36.

Shapiro, J. P., Burkey, W. B., Dorman, R. L., & Welker, C. J. (1996). Job satisfaction and burnout in child abuse professionals: Measure development, factor analysis, and job characteristics. *Journal of Child Sexual Abuse, 5,* 21–38.

Shapiro, J. P., Dorman, R. L., Burkey, W. B., & Welker, C. J. (1999). Predictors of job satisfaction and burnout in child abuse professionals: Coping, cognition, and victimization history. *Journal of Child Sexual Abuse, 7,* 23–42.

Thornton, P. I. (1992). The relation of coping, appraisal, and burnout in mental health workers. *Journal of Psychology, 126,* 261–271.

About the Authors

Rebekah L. Dorman, PhD, is a developmental psychologist and Vice President of Applewood Centers, Inc., a private, nonprofit behavorial health care agency in Cleveland, Ohio. She has worked in the field of human services for the past 20 years, focusing on developing and implementing programs for families at risk. Currently, she heads the division of Family and Child Development at Applewood, which includes home visiting programs, child care, foster care, adoption, and early childhood mental health services. In the course of her work, she has supervised staff in many different capacities, from line staff to program directors. Dorman is the senior author of *Planning, Funding, and Implementing a Child Abuse Prevention Project* (Child Welfare League of America, 1999), and she has authored numerous other publications on topics including parenting, youth violence, and job satisfaction. She has garnered Aegis Communicator, and Telly awards for videos she produced on children and families under stress.

Jeremy P. Shapiro, PhD, a clinical psychologist, is an adjunct faculty member in the Psychology Department and Mandel School of Applied Social Sciences of Case Western Reserve University. He is also a research consultant, trainer, and psychotherapist in private practice. His research and program development interests include burnout in the human services, youth violence prevention, child therapy methods, and mental health treatment outcome research. He has published numerous professional books and articles and has given trainings on these topics across the country. He is the author of the Peacemakers Program, a violence prevention intervention that was named a Promising Program for Safe, Disciplined, and Drug-free Schools by the U.S. Department of Education; that received the Governor's Community Peace Award from Ohio; and that received the Anisfield-Wolf Award from the Cleveland Foundation. Shapiro was Dorman's supervisor for six years, and she reports that he prevented slightly more burnout than he caused.